GREEK SHIPPING CLUSTER

Mauro Tommaso De Candia

INDEX

Executive Summary

1. Analysis of the country

1.1 Economic Structure

1.2 Elements of Greek Competitiveness

1.3 National Diamonds Analysis

1.4 Policy recommendations

2. Shipping Cluster Analysis

2.1 Overview of Shipping

2.2 History of Greek Shipping

2.3 Relative positioning in the global market

2.4 Mapping the Greek shipping cluster

2.4.1 Related industries

2.5 Cluster competitiveness

2.5.1 Financial performance

2.5.2 The role of the Greek government

2.5.3 Positive cluster spillovers

2.5.4 Value added to the Greek economy

2.5.5 Comparison across the region of EU

2.6 The Diamond Model

2.7 Recommendations

References

EXECUTIVE SUMMARY

Greece is a country that despite of its actual economic problems did experience an increase of its economy. This is probably thanks to the accession to the Eurozone. Greece entered in the Eurozone on January 2001 and it has provided the country of monetary stability. Greece depends of borrowings, so its growth rates could not be sustain in a long term. In consequence, the deficiencies in the country's competitiveness were masked.

This has some bad effects on the county:

- Poor exports of products and services.
- Absence of Foreign Direct Inversion (FDI).
- Lack of Innovation.

Greece has competitiveness problems in different areas, but the most important are related to the government. The country should try to gain in fiscal viability that should be a priority for the government. Despite on the economic problems that the Greece is suffering, there is a brilliant cluster in the country, the shipping cluster. Around 800 ship operators compose the large of Greece float cannot be surpassed by any other country in the world, its core. Shipping has traditionally been one of the key elements of the country economy since ancient times.

During the years, Greece shipping cluster has developed new ways to get a major contribution to global transportation & logistics in order to maintain the global leadership in the international shipping industry. Many factors have contributed the development of this industry in Greece.

In the country, there is a high rivalry thanks to the many small companies. There are also many companies created for collaboration. The tax regimen of the country is so favorable and networks for information are so strong. All this things seems to be key factors to contribute developing the cluster competitiveness, also the help that specialized maritime educational institutions give.

In the other hand, we should also mention the disadvantage that the country has comparing other countries like China and Japan, where the local demand for the cluster's services is much more bigger.

In conclusion, in the future the country should try to increase the benefit of the cluster. Greece should also try to promote the innovation on the sector to maintain its competitive advantage.

1. ANALYSIS OF THE COUNTRY

In this section, we will see the problems that in a way restrict Greek competitiveness. We will also give some few policy recommendations to help improving the competitiveness of the country. Despite to the problems that the crisis might cause in Greece economy and therefore to the shipping cluster, it offers a perfect opportunity to make some political reforms that might help improving Greece competitiveness.

1.1 Economic Structure

Generally, Greece is a developed country that its population is approximately 11.3 million people, and it is located in Southern Europe.

According to the Global Competitiveness Report 2013-2014, Greece is an innovative country. On the rating results, Greece is in the 91st place out of 148 nations

We should mention also that from 2012, Greece moved up two places, showing us its great development even on crisis. Here is a graphic taken from the Global Competitiveness Report 2013-2014, which describes generally the situation in Greece.

Stage of development

[Radar chart comparing Greece to Innovation-driven economies across: Institutions, Infrastructure, Macroeconomic environment, Health and primary education, Higher education and training, Goods market efficiency, Labor market efficiency, Financial market development, Technological readiness, Market size, Business sophistication, Innovation. Greece is at Stage 3: Innovation driven.]

Source: The Global Competitiveness Report of 2013-2014

As we can see in the graphic, Greece is similar to the innovative economies in Market size and Health and primary education, but Greece is so far away from the innovative economies in the rest of points so it should be improved in all the points that we can observe in the graphic.

We can find many doubtful factors for "doing business". We could mention that the most significant of them are the limited access to financing, insufficient government bureaucracy, tax regulations and policy instability.

It can be assigned that the Greek economic growth during the last two years is because of the entrance of the country to the European Union in 1981. Because of this, Greece has had the opportunity to take advantage of the transfers of the European Union and low labor costs, reaching high growth rates.

As we have said, Greece adopted the euro in 2001 and it increased the macroeconomic stability of the country with an average growth rate of 3.8% during the first 7 years.

After that period, Greece adopted another policy and instead increasing the exportations, the country increased the consumption (private and public) and housing investment. The interest rates fall down with the adoption of the euro, fueling private borrowing. This caused that the private sector debt level as a ratio of GDP increased from 25% in 2000 to 100% in 2009. The average of the investment rate was more or less the same to the euro zone, within this, the share of housing investment got unusual high levels.

The Greek exports were mainly around transportation (mostly shipping) and tourism. These clusters are in this way the most important with a weight of 40% of the exportations. There are many other clusters in Greece like agricultural products, and oil & gas.

1.2 Elements of Greek Competitiveness

The Greek economy is currently at a bad time since the crisis began in 2008. The Greek economic crisis occurred after the onset of the economic crisis in the United States in August 2007. Because of this crisis, Greece has issued large amounts of debt to finance the deficit. The level of debt has begun to cause concern in the early weeks of 2010. The situation worsened when it was discovered that the Conservative government had hidden for years, the real value of debt. The huge debt has prompted the government to make major cuts in public spending and because of this, the population has responded with numerous demonstrations and riots since the crisis began.

On 23 April 2010, the Greek government was forced to take a loan from the European Union, in what would be the first request to "save" the impossibility of sustaining the public debt. Despite the effort to reduce debt, the Greek government was forced to order another second rescue in the summer of 2011.

How we have seen, Greece suffers serious competitiveness problems. In the Global Competitiveness index, Greece is ranked 61 having 128 countries[1]. The situation is even more shading if we consider the income of Greece. If you look at Greece, stands out as the least competitive economy of European Union.

One of the most surprising data that we obtained after our analysis is that low competitiveness Greek suffers more where there is greater Starring government. Fiscal policy and administrative infrastructure stand out as the less competitive areas. This is directly related to the intervention of the government, as we can see, *(Institute for Strategy and Competitiveness)*, it is clearly ineffective.

The problem of business strategy and competitiveness lies in the participation of the government and the rigid rules of employment. FDI rules are also unfavorable. The only area in which Greece is better qualified is monetary policy, which is fully delegated to the European Central Bank

1.3 National Diamonds Analysis

The national diamond analysis for Greece illustrates the general image of the country based on the recent results of the GCI rankings. The participation of Greece in the European Union helps the country to manage a competitive value through Europe, but not the domestic factor conditions of the country

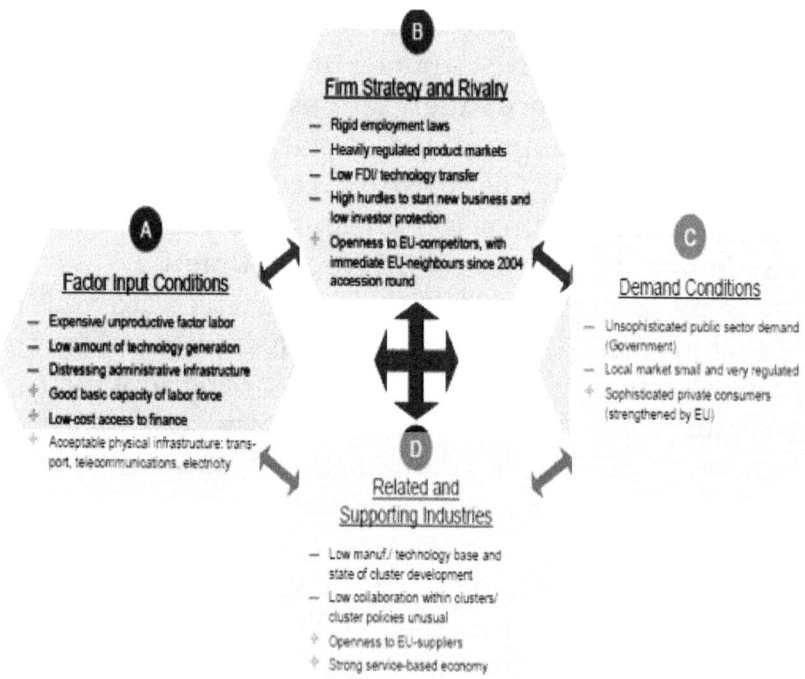

Source: Icaza, L., et al. (2009). The Greek shipping cluster. Harvard Business School.

Factor Input Conditions

Greece has shown a slight improvement during 2013-2014 compared to the year of 2012-2013. Ranked is now in 91st place instead of 96th as it was the previous year.

GCI 2012–2013		GCI 2013–2014	
Country/Economy	Rank/144	Country/Economy	Rank (out of 148)
Argentina	94	Moldova	89
Serbia	95	Namibia	90
Greece	96	Greece	91
Jamaica	97	Trinidad and Tobago	92
Gambia, The	98	Zambia	93

Source: Global Competitiveness Index 2012-2013 and 2013-2014

The Institutional environment of Greece shows us that there is no great development on labor markets and technological faculty (accordingly to recent statistical researches). Greece needs to change many things until to be able to reach the improvement that it wants. In particular, on labor markets, Greece is totally characterized of unproductivity. In addition, we should mention that the labor market's cost is far too high. All these show that there is a need to make labor markets more competitive and flexible as well. On the other hand, Greece also faces problems on adopting new technological generation systems even if its work force is educated enough to accept and use this kind of technology. Therefore, if Greece takes care of the above, it can survive from the crisis or at least can reduce the amount of loans and financial debts.

In addition, we should refer to the culture of Greeks. Corruption, especially in the political system, destroys the improvement of the country.

Firm Strategy and Rivalry

The employment laws are very rigid in Greece. This happens because government members are unable to agree on a common solution, as they have many disagreements about the way of governance. This situation in combination with the high rate of bureaucracy causes many problems relative to the regulation of the employment laws. The product markets are also heavily regulated and inflexible because of the previous reason. Because of this situation, in "the Doing Business" employing workers index, Greece has one of the lowest ranking among EU peers.

Ease of doing business

The following graph describes the "ease of doing business". As it seems, Greece has the lowest rate of doing business in comparison with the rest countries of Europe (Germany, Belgium, France, Austria, Spain and Italy). The rate of Greece is 100, considering that the regional Average is 29.

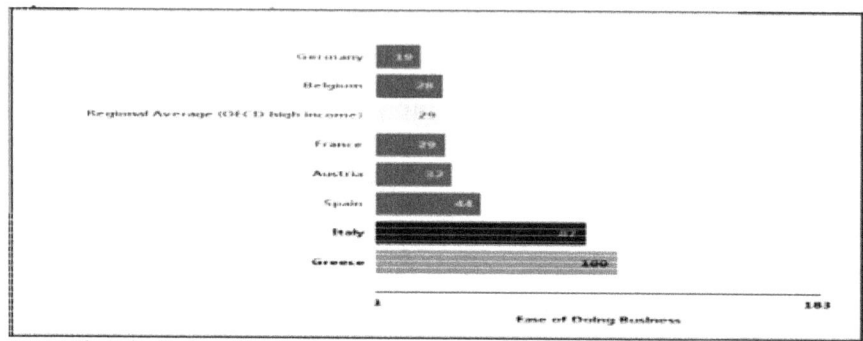
Source: The Doing Business 2012 Report.

It is measured the ease of starting a new business in the Greek economy by recording all the procedures that are officially required to begin and operate a company. In particular, requires 10 procedures, takes 10 days, costs 20,1% of income per capita and requires paid-in minimum capital of 22,8% of income per capita. The procedures are more than the OECD countries average, the cost is much more than the OECD countries average and the paid-in minimum capital is just a little more than the OECD countries average. Additionally, Greek firms increased their investments outside of Greece, making Greek net FDI flows negative in the recent years. While outward investment by Greek firms strengthens Greece's economic connections with the region and increases its importance as a regional hub, low levels of inward FDI reduce the potential to develop skills, upgrade clusters and innovate within Greece.

Demand conditions

Greece has a local market, which is small and very much regulated. The Greek economy is described by sectorial specialization with a business structure, in which traditional families are the owners of a high share of these enterprises. These kind of enterprises generate unsophisticated goods and services for local markets. Greek firms take the advantage of being member of the European market, one of the biggest and most sophisticated markets all over the world. Although Greek private consumers have a similar sophisticated demand as European consumers have, the demand by the Greek public sector is totally unsophisticated.

Greece's innovation performance is low, and Greece invests is very small in R&D.

Related and Supporting Industries
Although Greek firms have the advantage of EU access supplier base as well as a strong Greek service sector, the level of cluster development is low. The low level of cluster development is due to the fact that Greek firms have not introduce so much updated technology as in the rest of European countries. Moreover, the high level of unemployment in combination with low rate of investment in Greek companies makes it difficult for the country to develop competitive clusters through Europe. Greece does not have a coherent cluster policy, or strong institutions for collaboration. Greek performance is high in the areas that have access to the European suppliers in comparison with the low issues who deal with clusters. The identification of poorly performing clusters of economic activity within the Greek economy has significant policy implications. In conclusion, there is a need for developing a strategic vision for linking economic and technological planning.

1.4 Policy recommendations

In Greece, the economic problems are the direct effects of the recent crisis and fiscal consolidation is urgent. Many difficulties have been ongoing for many years, and after the crisis, Greece was more exposed than the other was. Greece has lost its value and international competitiveness. Therefore, the country should start taking steps to avoid poverty. Some recommendations may be useful for the recovery of the country.

Greece needs to increase the flexibility of the labor market, reduce unemployment, particularly among young people, and protect the work through a prudent legislation. The minimum wage does not act as a disincentive to the recruitment of young people. The chart below illustrates the unemployment rate for Greek age from 2004 to 2012. Apparently, the percentage of unemployed young people has increased during the years of 2004-2012:

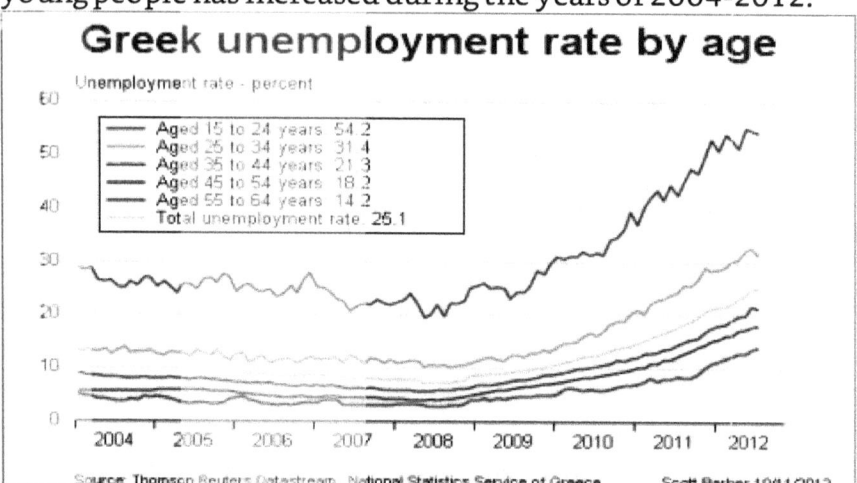

Furthermore, Greek governance must change tax laws. Poverty should be eliminated and more benefits should be offered to the work force of the country.

Competitiveness strategy, at this point, it is necessary to overcome economic crisis.

How Greece can make this strategy? By finding out to which economical cluster it has the competitive advantage over other countries. The answer is SHIPPING CLUSTER because of its special geographical position and climate advantages!

In addition, Greek governance should reduce the phenomenon of bureaucracy that is very high in Greece and makes all the procedures of any company difficult to be done! For this, Greek governance should adopt very strict methods, as well as, accepting the privatization of more companies.

To summarize, Greece needs growth of shipping cluster and privatization to the companies.

2. SHIPPING CLUSTER ANALYSIS

2.1 Overview of Shipping

Shipping is by the most important point of international trade as 90% of goods are transmitted over the sea and is substantial for connecting big sectors of the world's economy. Since 1734, shipping manufactures have met more than 20 boom-bust cycles. The most recent cycle started in 2004 and summited in 2008 before waning quickly at the onrush of the global financial crisis.

The shipping kinds are dry bulk carriers, tankers, cargo ships, container ships, cruise and ferries ships. There are around 50,000 merchant ships trading globally, transporting every category of cargo. The world navy is registered in over 150 nations, and manned by over a million seafarers of practically every nationality.

It is significant to refer to the fact that even the global economic crisis, shipping industry grew 4% in 2011 grading a 16% growth in ton-kilometers. Ships are long-range investments that can yield returns for 20 or 30 years, and trade will almost certainly raise during the life span of any given ship. While purchasing new-edition ships may seem contrasted in an oversupplied market, companies are informed that the capital cost of a ship plays a disproportionately large role in defining how profitable that ship will be. This means that shipping maybe has the response to the economic crisis. The difficult part of the shipping is to designate the ownership. A shipping that is named "Greek Shipping" means that Greek interests own this shipping. The location of the company is unconnected to the name of the shipping company. The flag is dependent only from the firm's ships in which is recorded.

2.2 History of Greek Shipping

The Greeks have a great history of transportation. The Greek people, more than anyone else, is mostly connected with the sea, especially economically. The endless coastline that covers 92 percent of the borders of Greece as natural harbors, deep coves, golden beaches and hundreds of picturesque islands. It was obvious that these beautiful landscapes have inspired the Greeks and instilled in them the love for the sea. The geographical position of Greece was an advantage because it is about half of the ancient Mediterranean, between Asia and Italy, near Egypt and Libya, and next to the other countries of the Balkans was at the crossroads of the oldest routes navigation. As a result, this situation has created the best conditions for the Greeks to become great men of transportation. The Greeks began their expedition in prehistory with the emergence and dominance of the fleet of Crete and to a lesser extent with the establishment of similar fleets of some cities in mainland Greece. Thus, the Cretans were the first who managed to build a large marina and conquer the Mediterranean.

The Greek shipping has been characterized by two elements over the last three centuries:

1) The strong link with family and morality;

2) The ability of Greek ship-owners to change their position depending on the economic environment and international politics.

At the beginning of the First World War, the Greeks had 475 steamers and 884 sailing ships of 1,001,116 gross tons. At the end of the war, 57.5 percent of their steam ships had been lost. After the Second World War, a large number of transport companies Greek moved to London because of the political situation.

The Greeks were not the maritime operators for thousands of years, but the modern transportation industry of the country did not take shape until the end of World War II. Then, the Greek ship-owners, led by Stavros Niarchos and Aristotle Onassis spotted the huge opportunity in the decision of the U.S. government to sell hundreds of surplus vessels for military transport at discounted prices.

The two men made their fortunes from their merchant fleet operations. In 1970, Piraeus in Athens started to become a global port. Shipping accounted for 18 billion euro Greek economy in 2008 and received transport account for about 6-8 percent of the GDP of Greece. Following the recent global economic crisis, the shipping income in Greece fell by 31.3 percent in the first eight months of 2009.

2.3 Relative positioning in the global market

Nicholas Tsakos, chief of Tsakos Energy Navigation (Greek shipping cluster) points out that generally Greek shipping has positive results on the country's economy.

Very important thing that should be mentioned is that Tasks Group establish Training Center in Athens as well as Maritime Researches.

The technology that is used is of the highest level (6th generation), powered by IBM.

A topic of great importance is that Greek economy could easily grow by 12,7 billion to 26 billion euros annually because of shipping cluster.

In 2009, shipping cluster offered 8,4 billion euros to Greece. However, shipping cluster does not only offer money to a period of economic crisis but it also offers a great reduction of unemployment.

Greece takes the second worldwide place on merchant fleet, 3rd place goes to Germany, 4th to China and 5th to US.

Greek ship-owners have more than 3000 ships and a total amount of 17% of work force in comparison with other countries.

Greek shipping has the largest share of total exported services, 65%.

Other countries that are big ship-exporters are Germany, China and Japan.

China takes the majority of shipbuilding orders because of its cheap shipyards costs.

During the last decades, Greek shippers show a great specialization on dry-bulk and container vessels.

Therefore, specialization with low cost of shipbuilding (china), are the factors that make Greece able to recover from this terrible economic situation!

Shipyards of China started to become even better not only because of their low costs but also in their quality. The prices that Chinese shipbuilders can offer, reach on 10%-15% lower than the average prices that shipbuilders from Japan and Korea are able to offer.

Korean yards still have the superior hand in building specified vessels, such as offshore oil-drill ships and liquefied natural-gas carriers. "But the Chinese are catching up fast", said XRTC's Managing Director George Xiradakis, who also advises China Development Bank.

"Shipping constitutes one of the sectors where Greece has a global competitive advantage. We can say indicatively that the average operational cost of the Greek-owned fleet is 23% more competitive than the global average" Camille Egloff-Ghicas, Head of BCG Shipping Practice for Southeastern Europe.

Despite the €300bn deficit and government bonds selling as trash, the Greek commercial shipping industry was still the strongest of the world. Greece has been a maritime nation since ancient years, and its ships still carriage about 15 per cent of global trade and constitute 18 per cent of the world's navy. After tourism, shipping is one of the pillars of the Greek economy.

2.4 Mapping the Greek shipping cluster

Which is the core of Greek shipping cluster?
The main core of Greek shipping cluster is bulk carriers and oil tankers. It is specialized more in bulk transportation of dry and liquid cargo. These ships reach the 95% of Greek merchant fleet and coastal ships (commercial, cruisers) reach the rest 5%.
In Greece, the amount of ship-companies is more than 800. Among them 4 are by the biggest ship-companies. These are:
1. Angelicoussis Group (7%)
2. Cardiff Marine (5%)
3. Tsakos Energy Navigation (4%)
4. Dynacom (3%)
The majority of ship-companies are placed in Piraeus, the largest harbor in Greece.

What about Maritime Greek services?
Maritime Greek services are over 1200. Large variation of individual and technical brand firms which are concentrated on technical ship faculty and ship design in Pireus. Maritime services include: Maritime works, Maritime R&D and consultancy, Shipping brokers and agency (290 firms), Specialized legal services (over 100 lawyers), Specialized finance (over 210 banks and firms), Underwriters and maritime insurance, Ports and security.

What we know about Maritime equipment and suppliers?
This group of companies includes ship equipment manufacturers and suppliers (400 firms) as well as machinery and engine repair firms (160). It is about ship repairing and engineering activities. Maritime equipment and suppliers include: Shipyards, Ship equipment manufacturers, Spare parts suppliers and Machinery and engine repair. Maritime equipment and suppliers faculty has low employment.

2.4.1 Related industries
<u>Fisheries and Fishing Equipment</u>: Greece is famous for being by

the countries with the biggest fishing fleet in the European Union. In 2002 total fisheries, production is counted at 99029 tons of a total value around 329270 EUROS.

<u>Coastal shipping</u>: (1892-1932) was a "perfect competition" period. However, the end of period was destructive. The problem of coastal shipping is that has a small amount of suppliers and on the other hand, a great number of users. As well as low level of knowledge and lack of good information.

<u>Ports and port authorities</u>: There is a huge list of ports and harbors, such as, Aegina, Antirrio, Heraklion, Igoumenitsa, Piraeus)

<u>Navy and coastguard</u>: Greek navy is considered as one of the Greek armed forces.

<u>Shipbuilding and Ship repair</u>: Few Greek companies deal with shipbuilding faculty.

These are:
1. Basileiades
2. Eleusis Shipyards
3. Hellenic shipyards
4. Co, Neorion

Only two of them are the largest: Hellenic Shipyards and Eleusis Shipyards.

The negative thing is that not many people that are employed.

<u>Greek Maritime education</u>: Greece has nine high level maritime academies. The training centers for engineers and master are two, like two for life saving, one for radio-communications and fire fighting and one for stewards. The traditional Maritime training contains food, books, free accommodation. In addition, the students apply three levels of education system. First, it is about the primary training for engineers. Secondly, it is about the practicing for the Navy (AEN). Third, Master Education level (ΚΕΣΕΝ). Although there are enough faculties for shipping work force training, many young people do not prefer to follow this kind of training centers because of the high level of bureaucracy. Many people claim that governance should give the right to individuals for building a private Maritime university. With this decision, we can reach the highest level of maritime competition.

POSIDONIA - THE INTERNATIONAL SHIPPING EXHIBITION. WHAT IS POSIDONIA EXHIBITION? Posidonia exhibition is an exhibition which going to take place at Metropolitan Expo Athens, Greece on June 2-6, 2014. Debates, social gatherings are some of the events that are going to take place on this great exhibition! Great deals done. Posidonia week is renowned for deals done in the exhibition. There are great deals for ship-owners and anyone that going to take part on this event.

2.5 Cluster competitiveness

2.5.1 Financial performance

As we know, Greece has the largest merchant fleet in the world, speaking in tons. However, China, Germany and Japan have gained much market share in the last decade. In the financial analysis, it does not have much information, since most of the Greek shippers are private. As for publicly traded companies, the Greek shipping companies outperform their peers during the current financial crisis, measured terms of return on average assets, the dividend yield and net profit margin. We can see it in *Capital IQ and Yahoo Finance*.

2.5.2 The role of the Greek government

If we look back to the history, the most important thing the government has done in the maritime sector has been the favorable tax and regulatory regime established in the 60s and 70s. The Greek Constitution guarantees the right of capital mobility for shipping companies. This has helped to reduce the level of uncertainty associated with investment costs. This encouraged the Greek ship-owners to return to their home, and in the last three decades is repatriated capital. The following provisions are included in the tax regime:

- Easy to apply a tax on tonnage instead of income tax for the vessels of Greek registration
    - No capital gains tax on the re-sale of the ships and no tax liens on the accumulated capital, thus promoting active participation in the second hand market.
    - Foreign shipping not have to pay taxes on income or have to spend any control over limited liability companies. The grouping in Pireop promotes this band.

The Greek government adopted an approach to regulatory intervention not flexible operation, endowments and foreign flag rules. This contrasts with the approach of the government in coastal navigation, which remains highly regulated.

Other measures taken by the Greek government to overcome the crisis:

- Application of a new package of additional measures to save 26,000 million euros until 2015
- Program of privatization of state assets, totaling 50,000 million euros
- Greece had plans to go back to the markets by early 2012, when I had to pay 27,000 million in interest on its debt.

2.5.3 Positive cluster spillovers

Traditionally, Greek shipping groups have been based on family and ethnic networks, but today most ship-owners come from non-traditional settings, thanks to the strength of employment and overflows within the grouping. The crossed between different companies nurture efforts experience. Employees from different areas of the grouping that was subsequently sent, may become so in-vessel managers. We can look for it in *Theotokas & Harlaftis, 2004*.

2.5.4 Value added to the Greek economy

Actually, the Greek shipping has no great influence on the Greek economy. Although it employs more than 100,000 Greeks and is an important source of income for reliable bank borrowers. Greek shipping companies have bought Greek debt two ways: corporate and sovereign. On the other hand, tax revenues it produces are not very high, due to the favorable treatment of this cluster enjoys. Greek ship-owners do not depend on the strength of the Greek economy dependent changes in international trade. Greek ship-owners are said to be the "drivers in the world"

Thanks to economic diversification undertaken by the country, the industry has replaced agriculture as a second source of income after services (about 20% of GDP). The main sectors are electronics, transport equipment, clothing and construction. Greece is the largest operator of the world. The service sector accounts for three quarters of GDP and employs two-thirds of the labor force. Tourism provides an essential source of income for himself and brings 11% of GDP. Merchant shipping accounts for 10% of GDP[2].

2.5.5 Comparison across the region of EU

Although Greece possesses the world's largest fleet, is positioned at number six in terms of value added. Regarding the creation of employment is located at number four. As we can see in *Policy Research Corporation, 2008* this is because Greece only produces 3% of the total value added of the population, whereas others EU countries produce much more.

As seen above, Greece has a low value added. This is mainly due to two reasons. Mainly, all companies that support fleets are small. Meanwhile, the fleet has little shipments benefit with relation to its size. *(Policy Research Corporation, 2008)* As we have seen in Greece in productivity very low in general. However, productivity in the ocean transportation is much more concentrated. In other countries, the value added is more dispersed in maritime port, shipbuilding and marine equipment.

The contribution of the merchant marine is not very high in Greece. This is because there are no side effects in shipments due to the small size of the companies that support shipments. It may also be because the Greek merchant navy is highly specialized in the bulk markets and not developed in terms of innovation. Neither has added value at the time of packaging and transportation specialized merchandise.

2.6 The Diamond Model

The international shipping industry has undergone many changes over the last thirty years. Nevertheless, Greece has maintained a leading position in all these years. This section aims to examine the factors that have contributed to this success, using as an analysis tool The Diamond Model of Professor Porter[3].

Overall, the diamond cluster shows a favorable environment for shipping companies in Greece. The success of the cluster is mainly due to historically favorable conditions and a strong business strategy and rivalry. On the other hand, the growth of the cluster was not together with the development of strong related industries. The local demand conditions have a minor effect on the cluster, because it draws its demand from international markets.

<u>Context for firm strategy and rivalry</u>: The rivalry between the companies belonging to the cluster has improved competitiveness and increased efficiency. The fragmentation of companies has also increased the flexibility of the cluster in a market where conditions change, by varying the number of firms in the cluster between the different phases of the global economic cycle. Government policies in favor of the regulation and taxation play an important role in improving the competitiveness of the cluster. Nevertheless, a low value added to the economy in the cluster indicates the absence of activities based on innovation by firms, with a strong dependence on more and more on cost reduction as a competitive advantage.

<u>Factor input conditions</u>: The long history of Greek shipping cluster and the strong connection of the population with the culture and maritime traditions have facilitated the accumulation of significant expertise in operational management. Marine academies and institutes of technical education provide highly skilled labor available for the cluster. However, there has been a net reduction

in the shipping labor, although this decline has mainly affected low-skilled workers who have been attracted to other types of better-paid jobs.

Related and supporting industries: Demand from the shipping cluster has established a wide network of related industries in Greece, but these industries are not enough competitive internationally. Because of the poor performance in these areas, the benefit of Greek maritime sector to the GDP of the country is significantly lower than in countries in which the shipping sector is much smaller.

Demand conditions: The Greek tradable sector is very tiny and there is very little local demand to support the industry. Greek shipping has prospered due to the rapid growth of world trade and above all because of the increased demand for raw materials from emerging countries.

COMPETITIVE ADVANTAGES	COMPETITIVE DISADVANTAGES
CONTEXT FOR FIRM STRATEGY AND RIVALRY	
Fragmented and highly competitive market	No innovation
Low barriers to entry	
Favorable tax law	
FACTOR INPUT CONDITIONS	
Accumulated expertise in operational management	Reduction in the shipping labor
Marine academies and institutes of technical education	
Strong connection between the population and the maritime cultures	
RELATED AND SUPPORTING INDUSTRIES	
Wide network of related industries	Not enough competitive internationally
DEMAND CONDITIONS	
Increased demand for raw materials from emerging countries	Very little local demand

2.7 Recommendations

Based on the analysis above, we identify four key challenges and propose the following recommendations to overcome them.

Increase externalities to the rest of the economy: In line with our recommendations on a national basis, we recommend to attract foreign investment in the most sophisticated maritime cluster (ports, maritime services) where Greece currently has a weak presence. Ports of Piraeus and Thessaloniki should be marketed as a regional transportation hub between the Balkans and the Middle East. The recent operational leasing of the port of Piraeus to the COSCO, a Chinese company, and the privatization of the Skaramangas shipyard to Abu Dhabi Mar, a holding company in the United Arab Emirates, are steps in the right direction. We recommend deregulating the coastal navigation and encouraging further investment in the sector. Greece has the potential to develop its tourism industry by exploiting its strengths as a hub for cruise ships in the Mediterranean Sea. We recommend encouraging the creation of cluster-based organizations to complement the existing industry associations. Give these organisms voice at the negotiating table and encourage them to identify policy recommendations relevant to the cluster.

Increase Greek transport competition: We recommend increasing competition in the Greek transport cluster. The government should undertake new initiatives to attract international transport companies in Piraeus, using the existing favorable tax treatment. The creation of a center for maritime transport in Athens and a campaign of seeking investment organized by the government can be undertaken.

Upgrade educational quality: The decline in local labor is in part due to the availability and ease of supply of cheap labor teams from low-cost countries. Lower the cost of unskilled Greek labor is not feasible. The focus should be to ensure a sufficient supply of highly skilled labor. The government should invest resources in the creation of new institutions and educational programs with a focus on building managerial skills to complement the current focus on technical skills. Innovative business practices will be encouraged by the sustainability of the competitive advantage of the cluster from which it is promoted.

<u>Lack of local demand</u>: We recommend negotiating favorable tax agreements between Greece and competing centers such as China and Japan to promote the establishment of subsidiaries of Greek shipping companies in these countries. Greece can offer operational expertise and knowledge in exchange for greater access to these markets.

REFERENCES:

- Slides from Prof. Fernando Giuseppe Alberti and Prof. Emanuele Pizzurno.
- Porter, M., E. (1998). On Competition. Boston: Harvard Business School Press.
- http://www.pwc.com/gr/en/industries/shipping.jhtml
- Schwab, K., (2013). The Global Competitiveness Report 2013 – 2014. World Economic Forum. http://www3.weforum.org/docs/WEF_GlobalCompetitivenessReport_2013-14.pdf
- http://en.wikipedia.org/wiki/Greek_government-debt_crisis
- Icaza, L., et al. (2009). The Greek shipping cluster. Harvard Business School.
- The doing business 2012 report. The World Bank & IFC. http://www.doingbusiness.org/~/media/FPDKM/Doing%20Business/Documents/Annual-Reports/English/DB12-FullReport.pdf
- http://www.portafolio.co/internacional/grecia-sigue-tomando-medidas-su-crisis
- http://comercioexterior.banesto.es/es/elija-su-mercado-objetivo/perfiles-de-paises/grecia/economia?type_d_utilisateur=aucun&

---

[1] Global Competitiveness Index. 128 countries ranked
[2] http://comercioexterior.banesto.es/es/elija-su-mercado-objetivo/perfiles-de-

paises/grecia/economia?type_d_utilisateur=aucun&

[3] Porter, M., E. (1998). On Competition. Boston: Harvard Business School Press

www.ingramcontent.com/pod-product-compliance
Lightning Source LLC
Chambersburg PA
CBHW070908220526
45466CB00005B/2175